" For me, 'What's Right, not Who's Right' reinforces the importance of leading in an authentic, curious, courageous, optimistic, and empathetic way. This is the formula for meaningful and transformational change. We must be purposeful in doing what's right.

When it comes to improved voting experience, 'what's right' is a combination of forces. We need an intentional, powerful balance among pro-voter policies, voter-centric processes, and effective, tamper-free technology. Each of these forces are helpful, but in combination they are transformational.

Please accept the gift of this book (thank you to the author, Bob Tipton, for making it possible) as a nudge for all of us to remember to keep 'what's right' in front as we move forward in our work for our citizens.

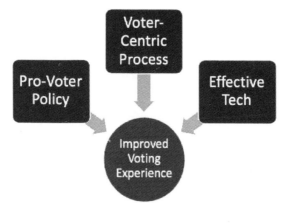

Amber McReynolds, executive director for the Vote at Home Institute (voteathome.org), and former director of elections for the City and County of Denver. 🐦 @AmberMcReynolds

What's Right

- not -

Who's Right

A Simple Shift to Regain
Our Humanity and Heal
Our Relationships—
at Home and at Work

Robert S. Tipton

AS

What's Right, Not Who's Right:
A Simple Shift to Regain Our Humanity and Heal Our
Relationships—at Home and at Work
Published by Alden-Swain Press
Denver, Colorado

Library of Congress Control Number: 2017913861

ISBN: 978-0-9825900-9-6

Business and Economics: Conflict Resolution and Mediation
Self-Help: Communication and Social Skills

Edited by: Kathy Nelson
Cover artwork by: Victoria Wolf
Book design by: Andrea Costantine
Author photo credit: Kokoro Photography
Book concept catalyst by: Patricia Pearce

QUANTITY PURCHASES: Schools, companies, professional groups,
clubs, and other organizations may qualify for special terms when
ordering quantities of this title. For information, email bulksales@
aldenswain.com.

For our elected officials—may you find the courage and patience to seek answers rooted in "what's right" and not "who's right." We need your compassionate leadership and wise decision-making.

CONTENTS

INTRODUCTION

It infuriates me to be wrong
when I know I'm right.

—Molière

Far too much time and energy are wasted in the world today because we are mired in endless debates about who's right while bickering, politicking, and posturing. It's such a waste because there's a completely different approach available to us—a simple shift, a change of thought pattern and behavior that has the potential to end the world's madness, to heal our relationships, and to regain our humanity (both individually and collectively).

It's available—right now. If we'll only look.

No, it's not some utopian mumbo jumbo, some "Stepford Wives-esque," robotic approach to shut down conflict and to make people go along. And no, it's not some religion, doctrine, dogma, or chemical. No drugs, no brainwashing, no requirements to "be saved."

It's something very, very different.

It's this: let's focus on "what's right" instead of "who's right."

In the thirty-plus years I've been working in the field of organizational development, transformational change, disruptive strategy, and cultural intervention, I've found the shift to "what's right" is the single most powerful change agent of them all. It's simple; however, that doesn't mean it's *easy*. Difficulties aside, I believe we can do a much better job when it comes to treating one another with dignity and respect—even when we disagree. Or maybe *especially* when we disagree. We're losing our humanity because we're addicted to "being correct" instead of "being connected."

Now, don't get me wrong. I don't think human nature is perfectible. We've been trying to change our nature for *centuries* through philosophy, religion, and such with some benefits here and there. However, most of our efforts fall short. After all, people are messy creatures who have all kinds of issues and imperfections—and we have opinions, attitudes, personalities, and egos. We aren't alike. Nor should we be alike. However, despite our differences, we can still be aligned.

That's what this book is about. It's about getting messy human beings to choose to be aligned in the midst of disagreement and differences of opinion.

Yes, the world can be a hard place—some things that people do to one another shock and stun us.

Just watch the news on any given day, and you can see members of the fringes of our society hurting and killing one another. In my work as an organizational change consultant, I all too often see mean, ugly, violent behaviors. However, these behaviors are often rooted in pain, worthiness issues, fear, and other "unprocessed suffering." The older I get, the more I realize that ugly responses to ugly behavior just create more ugliness, and the wise teachings of our elders are correct. Gandhi said, "Be the change you want to see." Here's what this means to me: If we want more love, peace, understanding, and healing in the world, we need to *be* love, *be* peace, *be* understanding, and *be* healing. Oh—and something I think Gandhi might have said as a footnote—"Be the change you want to see, even when it's hard, even when it's inconvenient, and even when you risk ridicule and possible violent reactions." There's a new way to look at this idea, true?

The single most powerful way to *be* all the things I mentioned above is to shift your consciousness, your thinking, the lens through which you see the world. Focus on *what's right, not who's right,* and you start to *be* those things. No question, it takes a certain kind of leader to have the patience to search for what's right instead of pushing the who's right button. "Because I said so" didn't work when we were children; why should we think it would work with adults? Leaders with this kind of patience don't think less "of" themselves; they just think less "about" themselves. Their mantra? "The needs of the many outweigh the egos of the few." Or stated another way, these kinds of leaders take situations seriously, but not themselves. *Be* the change you want to see—great advice. Let's try it.

To get into and *stay* in the energy of "what's right, not who's right," there's a list of insights I've found to be helpful (I'll dig into each in more detail in subsequent chapters):

- Some suffering is often needed before transformation is possible.
- See the value in our collective humanity.
- Recognize that it's more important to be connected than to be correct.
- Two wrongs never create a right.

- Be kind; everyone is struggling with something.
- Humanize rather than demonize "the other."
- Manage the energy *you* bring to the situation.
- Focus on interests, not positions.
- Keep "what's right" in front.
- Heal yourself so you can be a healing force in the world.

By doing these things, we leverage the power in "what's right" instead of dealing with the toxicity of "who's right," and the world around us transforms. We rethink our thinking and reimagine our leadership style as a result. Plan on it!

1

Unfortunately, Suffering Often Precedes Transformation

But what about the things we're all wrong about?
What about ideas that are so accepted and
internalized that we're not even in a position
to question their fallibility? These are ideas so
ingrained in the collective consciousness that it
seems foolhardy to even wonder if they're potentially
untrue. It is impossible to examine questions we
refuse to ask. These are the big potatoes.

—Chuck Klosterman,
But What If We're Wrong?

They had that stereotypical government vibe about them. Dark suits, white shirts, style-free ties, sensible shoes, six-dollar haircuts.

Helping to further set the mood was the fact that they brought along a chain and padlock with them, as well as a notice with the word "Seized" in red, 120-point font. They were in the process of attaching both to the door of my company when I arrived.

When I woke up that morning, I thought it was going to be just another normal day as a struggling entrepreneur. I had no idea that I'd encounter a pair of humorless, robotic IRS agents when I came to work.

I'll fast-forward through the "oh shit" conversation I had with myself, as well as the stammering, pleading "I had no idea" vomit of verbiage I threw at them both. Suffice it to say, my twenty-nine-year-old mind was racing, my blood pressure was skyrocketing, and I was thrust into a desperate plea to stave off a death sentence for my business.

Yes—eventually (after what seemed like hours but was probably only about six or eight minutes)—agents "unfriendly" and "unfeeling" finally shared with me the basis for their mission that morning. I had a problem—a big problem.

It turns out that our "business administrator," due to cash flow shortages, had just been paying net payroll for several months. In other words, the IRS had never received the withholding we should have been paying it. The federal government is both unfriendly and unfeeling when you mess with withholding taxes. Imagine that!

My unsophisticated, ignorant, and plain poor approach to running my business had caught up with me. I'd trusted the wrong people and had abdicated my responsibilities as the owner.

I was screwed. Or so I thought.

Then something incredibly simple turned the whole situation around—almost immediately. You see, IRS agents are trained and prepared for belligerent, angry, low-accountability responses when they take their business-seizure show on the road. What they're not expecting is this: vulnerability, authenticity, contrition, and flexibility.

I wasn't trying to not pay taxes. I wasn't trying

to avoid my responsibility. I was blissfully ignorant (and a bad business manager at the time), but down deep, I was a rule-following, high-integrity person.

Here's the bottom line. Once I realized what my situation truly entailed, I surrendered to it. I stopped trying to convince the agents of anything. I accepted the reality that was in front of me. Then the next big thing happened. I took full accountability for what had happened and requested, in as selfless a manner as I could muster, some time to work out a "both-and" solution to everything.

I asked for the opportunity to *both* keep the doors open *and* find a way to make things right with the IRS.

After a few terse phone calls with their supervisors, some supersecret hallway conversations between the agents, and some scribbling on their low-bidder-manufactured yellow pads, "unfriendly" and "unfeeling" had a response to my proposal.

"Yes, you may keep operating your business. *And* you will agree to a comprehensive audit of all your business operations over the past two years. Plus, you will enter into a binding legal agreement—including the requirement to guarantee repayment of your tax liability through your personal assets." Or something like that. That was more than twenty-five years ago now, but those are the highlights.

The next six months were the most challenging of my professional career, but they were also the most educational. I learned (and lived) the difference between "saying" you're committed and *being* committed. I had to make some *very* difficult decisions, including the need to be fully transparent. I also found a new respect for myself when it came to doing the right thing, the right way.

More importantly, I pulled my head out of my "I'm a twenty-something entrepreneur, and this is *fun!*" thinking, and I became open, vulnerable, and genuinely committed to learning what, how, and when to do what we needed. It was time to do the right thing and not be stuck on justifying my position or assigning blame. Clearly, I needed to listen.

Yes, this is a true story, and yes, we repaid every cent to the government.

Questions, Insights, Implications

1. Describe a situation when you needed to just shut up and listen. No justifying, no pleading, no trying to convince someone that you were right—just a time your mouth needed to close, and your ears needed to open. How did you feel?

2. When have you felt a strong sense of accomplishment and pride as a result of you doing the right thing—even when it was extremely difficult?

3. What value might you see in offering to be contrite, vulnerable, and truly remorseful in a situation where you've wronged someone else?

Take a moment—by yourself or with your spouse, friends, coworkers, teammates, or staff—to reflect on these questions. Give yourself room to be willing to be wrong, to be open to new perspectives, and to find answers in the most unusual places. Are there examples you are able to cite where these study questions have been applicable for you? Do you disagree with me in terms of what I've shared about them? Look deeply, but keep this "rule" in mind: With yourself and with others—as you look at your perspectives and feelings about these items—make sure you're looking through the lens of "what's right" and not "who's right." I expect you'll gain new insights immediately as a result.

GETTING TO "WHAT'S RIGHT," NOT "WHO'S RIGHT"

There is a very, very good chance that our understanding of gravity will not be the same in five hundred years. In fact, that's the one arena where I would think that most of our contemporary evidence is circumstantial, and that the way we think about gravity will be very different.
—Brian Greene, Ph.D., (chairman, World Science Festival; professor, Columbia University)

The necessity of "being right"—often at the expense of someone else—creates all kinds of problems in the world, and it has for centuries. However, it seems like we've reached an epidemic stage at this point in the world where the need to "be right" no longer is just an annoying urge leading to debate, discussion, and maybe going home and being upset for a while. Instead, it's taking an ugly turn. It's been brewing for the last few years, especially coming to a head here in the United States with our national politics, our two-party system, and the resulting extremism shown on the nightly news.

What's the endgame for this trend? We'll lose our humanity. Even today, we're losing a sense that we're all in this together, that we share this little blue ball in the middle of space, and that we have some shared challenges as a species related to taking care of it. Rather than looking at "what's right" for us collectively, we are creating political infighting, greed, family dysfunction, and domestic terrorism. The debate over the words "climate change" astounds me. Why can't we just get to "what's right" without the need to focus on "who's right"? It isn't a political question; it's about Earth, and there's no Planet B. I frankly don't care about the disagreement concerning the causes of climate change. Let's get to the "what's right" question and start *doing* something about it!

We can't simply disagree any longer, it seems. *Someone* has to be right, and that means everyone else needs to be wrong. Want some examples? Think of white supremacists, the KKK, and neo-Nazis on the streets of Charlottesville, Virginia. Think of the shooting of a congressman and three others at a charity baseball team practice in Alexandria, Virginia. Both events should be unacceptable in our culture—and to nearly *everyone* they are. However, rather than looking at the subject from a viewpoint of "what can we do about it together", the debate has devolved into name-calling, finger-pointing, and messages of "I'm right; you're wrong." We criticize one person for not getting the message right about denouncing the event while we vilify others because of their inaction. We're damned if we do, damned if we don't—because we're putting our energy into the wrong things.

Let's do a little "what if" here for a moment. What if we took a countercultural approach to this whole subject? Let's get shifted around to think about the notion of *what's right*. In other words, let's look at the things that connect us as opposed to the things that separate us. Let's look at how we share common interests instead of where our positions need to be defended. Let's find places where we are similar as opposed to being dissimilar.

In her book *Anatomy of the Spirit*, author Caroline Myss challenges the reader to take the major faiths of the world and stack them up on top of one another. She asks us to look at what the followers of these faiths believe at their core, the things that those faiths really stand for. By stacking them all up like a layer cake, turning the whole thing on its side and looking through it, you discover that the core essence of all the major faiths in the world is very, very similar.

Yes, there's stuff on the outside, the fringes and so on, that we can debate, but the similarities outweigh the differences by a wide margin. One example? Virtually *every* culture, in every location across the world, has some version of the Golden Rule. It's a basic truth for humanity. As the old saying goes, if it's true somewhere, it's true everywhere. No question we share far more similarities than differences.

How might this dynamic play out in business or organizational life?

I work as an organizational development consultant and find myself in countless meetings with leadership teams wrestling with strategy, culture, and operations. Recognizing the impact of ego, strong personalities, balance-of-power issues, and such things, I like to start each workshop with a series of "agreements together." (Note: Some may call them "ground rules," but I don't like the energy implied by the term "ground rules." I like the two words "agreements" and "together" because both words are positive, and they have an active choice implied in them—"we choose to agree, together.") You can find the entire list of agreements together, along with some description about them here (www. teamtipton.com/agreements-together), but the one I want to concentrate on is this one: "We'll take the situation seriously, but not ourselves. We'll focus on what's right, not who's right."

Because these groups tend to be made up of highly educated, successful, and really intelligent people, those people also tend to have strong personalities and sizable egos. In addition, they tend to come from professional disciplines such as engineering, law, medicine, and so on. But something is often missing from their training or experience. They usually just "assume" that they should be able to get along because, hey, they're professionals! In my experience, the more training someone has, the less often that person is actually well skilled in the art of human interaction. (OK, that's my bias, but it tends to be true!)

Anyway, here's how I start these meetings. I say, "Because we're going to take the situation seriously, but not ourselves, I need to say a few things. I don't really care about your education. I don't care about your position on the organization chart. I don't care how much money you make or how long you've worked here. Unless you're applying your skills, knowledge, and expertise to 'what's right,' it's irrelevant." Pause. I continue, "If any of you feel the need to 'be right'—particularly at someone else's expense—I'll call you out. If you persist in your need to 'be right,' you and I will have a separate conversation in the hallway." Another pause.

I let it sink in and look from face to face around the room.

Generally, I get some stunned facial expressions that seem to say, "Well, this is going to be a different meeting!" or "This won't be the same as it's always been," or "Who asked *this* guy to lead the meeting?" That said, I have never had anyone outright challenge me, and I think the reason is that at some deep level most people hunger for the chance to have a meeting where there's no politicking, no positioning, and no "alpha dog" behaviors. Maybe it's because I'm six feet six inches in bare feet and have a deep voice. Maybe. But other members of my team have given the same message to leadership teams with similar results. The message gets received, and people agree to focus on what's right.

What happens next? In my experience, they consider someone else's perspective before defending their own. Even for a moment they tend to humanize the person with whom they're working, and they're willing to see a different viewpoint and put their position to the side. Strong leaders operating from this perspective don't think less *of* themselves. They just think less *about* themselves. It's transformational all by itself.

Questions, Insights, Implications

1. What evidence do you see that we have a worldwide epidemic of people needing to be right?

2. When have you seen challenges in your own life, community, and so on associated with "who's right" (wars, political infighting, greed, family divisions, terrorism)?

3. Can you envision what the results might be of setting expectations through "agreements together" before meetings start? Before decisions are made?

Again, reflect on these questions, and allow yourself to be wrong and to be open to new perspectives. By doing so, you'll likely find new insights in the most unexpected places.

3

LOSING OUR HUMANITY: HOW DID WE GET HERE?

Of all the things we are wrong about, this idea of error might well top the list. It is our meta-mistake; we are wrong about what it means to be wrong. Far from being a sign of intellectual inferiority, the capacity to err is crucial to human cognition. Far from being a moral flaw, it is inextricable from some of our most humane and honorable qualities: empathy, optimism, imagination, conviction, and courage. And far from being a mark of indifference or intolerance, wrongness is a vital part of how we learn and change. Thanks to error, we can revise our understanding of ourselves and amend our ideas about the world.

—Kathryn Schulz, *Being Wrong: Adventures in the Margin of Error*

Once again, all you need to do is turn on the evening news (or your favorite online news feed, podcast, or social media outlet), if you're so brave to do that anymore, and you'll get a sense of how we're losing our humanity. Pick whatever topic, in whatever country, state, or city, and you'll see some stunning similarities. It's amazing to me how people are so eager to debase one another, call one another names, and call people's integrity into question. The media we consume is becoming more mean-spirited, less tolerant, and much less forgiving—and we as a species are following along.

How did we get here? It's been a progression, and I have a theory about it. As the world gets more complex and our connections to the world become more virtual, we seem to have retreated into our shells—where we can stand back and judge, criticize, condemn, be snarky, and name-call. It's a bit like the dynamic we experience in our cars, where many of us feel far freer to shout, spout expletives, and give angry, nonverbal feedback to those around us in other cars. We'd *never* do that (OK, some of us would) without the car around us (again, the shell).

The anonymity of web browsers gives us the same kind of shell—this one virtual—and we experience the same kind of dynamic.

We've become absolutely fixated on our need to be right about things, and somehow if we're perceived as being wrong, there's something wrong with us as individuals. Our identities are tied up in the ability to be perceived as being right.

Well, there's a TED Talk for that. I like watching TED Talks, and one of my favorites, by a woman named Kathryn Schulz, is called "On Being Wrong." Schulz begins her talk with a question for the audience. She asks, "How does it feel when you're wrong?" People in the audience shout out answers like "Embarrassing!" or "Frustrating!" or "Shameful!" She pauses, ever so slightly, and then says, "No, that's how it feels when you *realize* that you're wrong. How does it feel when you're wrong? It feels like you're right."

She's absolutely right. We don't know that we're wrong—we think we're right! Furthermore, we don't seem to question what we're saying. Often we repeat a post on Facebook, Twitter, or some "news source" without checking. Whole websites (Snopes. com, for example) have been built just to debunk all the misleading, inaccurate, downright wrong information out there. Even when someone quotes Snopes (and other websites) as a rebuttal to a comment on a post, I find it fascinating the number of people who *still* want to believe that the inaccurate (OK, downright *wrong*) statement is right. We've lost our curiosity. We've lost our ability to discern and dig in. We don't think critically, and we certainly have no patience to seek alternative viewpoints. Like Schulz says in her book, we are wrong about the whole notion of being wrong!

What are some examples of where we'll continue to describe something that's not true? How about these simple, relatively innocuous items: misheard lines from movies and TV shows. For example, the *Star Wars* character Darth Vader *never* said, "Luke, I am your father." And *Dragnet*'s Joe Friday *never* said, "Just the facts, ma'am." But, we think that both Darth Vader and Joe Friday said what we think they said, and we perpetuate the "wrongness," believing we are right. It's the land of "alternative facts."

By the way, the dialog in *Star Wars* is this:

Vader: "Obi Wan never told you what happened to your father."

Luke: "He told me enough! He told me you killed him!"

Vader: "No, I am your father."

The need to be right—or to hang on to our perceived correctness (which may be proven wrong at some point in the future)—causes us to do some really strange things at times. Depending on our need to be right, when someone disagrees with us, a progression of three reactions and countering responses may occur:

1. If people disagree with us, well, our response might be that they're just ignorant. Let's give them "the facts" (as we see them) and then expect them to agree.

2. However, even after getting "the facts" from us, they may still disagree. "Yes, I see the information you've shared, but I still don't agree," they might say. When that happens, we might say, "Well, you're just stupid."

ROBERT S. TIPTON

3. Then those people might say, "No, no, no. I have your information. I understand your information. But I still don't agree with you." The next reaction might be this: "Well, then, you're evil."

This three-step progression happens *every* day—on social media in particular. Have you ever posted a somewhat "controversial" Facebook status update? "What's on your mind, Bob?" Have your post threads ever been hijacked by people with an ax to grind about a particular topic? First, they act as if you're ignorant; you must not have the facts. So they give you the facts or try to convince you of their viewpoint. And you say, "No, no, no, I have the facts. I still disagree with you."

"Well, you're just stupid," they say.

"No. I have the facts. I understand them, and I'm not an idiot."

"Well—then—you're *evil*!" When you become evil, you are to be eliminated, eradicated from the situation. Block, unfriend, snark. Sound familiar? All too familiar in my experience.

It can get toxic quickly.

It gets toxic because we've lost our humanity, and that's because we're unwilling any longer to be able to be wrong in a situation. We're so wrapped up in this notion of being right that we can't see our own humility, our own vulnerability, our own "wrongness." If we can't see that in ourselves, how can we see it in someone else?

Again, watch Kathryn Schulz's video. She does a great job of making this dynamic *very* real. How does it feel when you're wrong? It feels like you're right. Are we willing to be wrong? Until that's true, we're unable to regain our own humanity.

Questions, Insights, Implications

1. What are the causes behind our tendency to tend to render instant judgment without healthy curiosity?

2. What are your views about the acceptability of "alternative facts"?

3. Have you seen examples of the "ignorance, stupidity, evil progression" in conversations you've had with others?

Again, reflect on these questions, and allow yourself to be wrong and to be open to new perspectives. By doing so, you'll likely find new insights in the most unexpected places.

4

It's More Important to Be Connected Than to Be Correct

When we stop caring about what people think, we lose our capacity for connection. When we become defined by what people think, we lose our willingness to be vulnerable. If we dismiss all the criticism, we lose out on important feedback, but if we subject ourselves to the hatefulness, our spirit gets crushed.

—Brené Brown

I have a dilemma for you, and like many dilemmas, it's a false one. (In other words, it's not really a dilemma, but I'm making it seem like one.) Here you go. Pick one.

You can be right, or you can be happy. Choose.

Now, consider how quickly you picked "be happy." I know that's the one you chose, and I think most of us really believe that. However, the behavior I see in the world tells me that we actually choose "right" far more often than "happy." Want evidence? How many people do you know who will hold a grudge for *decades* just so that they can be justified in being right about a situation? Or how many people will stay stuck in a horrible job or a dysfunctional relationship because they need to be right about being "safe"?

One of my favorite writers is Brené Brown, who also has one of the *most* frequently viewed TED Talks of all time, with about thirty-one million views ("The Power of Vulnerability" at www. ted.com/talks/brene_brown_on_vulnerability). In it, she describes herself as a "shame researcher." She tells us—pretty directly—that our most basic human need revolves around connection. We deeply need connection to others. However, we sabotage ourselves regularly in getting connected because *real* connection is based on vulnerability. We are terrible about owning our shortcomings, flaws, and places we see ourselves coming up short because somehow we won't "stoop to be vulnerable" in order to get past our own image of ourselves and build real connections with others as a result. I see misery, shame, loneliness, and depression all the time in others (even myself at times) because we stink at vulnerability.

As a result, our basic need for connection is missed. We're not able to make those connections because the individual we bring to the conversation isn't real. It's a made-up facade, a persona.

Think about going on a first date. I've been married to my high school sweetheart since we were twenty years old. It's been a long time since we went on our first date! So you're going to have to help me here when it comes to first-date preparation. What do you spend time doing? For us guys, and I'm going to generalize here, we will spend a significant amount of time cleaning the car. We'll take it to a "spa for cars," and they'll wash, wax, primp, polish, vacuum, and deodorize until our "mobile image machine" is perfectly put together. We'll shower— we may get a new shirt, and we may get some new hair products—but most of our attention is on the *car*. For women (again, not only am I generalizing, I'm also projecting here), I'm guessing you spend a considerable amount of time making sure *you're* put together—the right hair, makeup, nails, shoes, handbag. *You* want to have the right combination of looks.

Then the first-daters send their images out on the date to see how it goes.

So how did it go? Did you *really* connect, or were you more interested in being correct? Interesting question, no? From what I see, *most* first dates are somewhere on the unbearable to disastrous scale because "you" weren't really there. You were someplace else; you sent your persona instead. Getting connection—that's where joy is. That's where true fulfillment is. That's where there are feelings of being valued and important and making a difference for others.

Do you want to have the world work a little bit better? Do you want relationships to work a little bit better? Do you want to make better decisions? Do you want to feel more connected? Get connected. Be vulnerable and send your real self into situations.

Questions, Insights, Implications

1. What tradeoffs do you see related to the following idea: You can be right, or you can be happy—choose one.
2. Watch "The Power of Vulnerability" TED Talk. What themes from Brené Brown's talk speak to you most deeply? (Go to www.ted.com/talks/brene_brown_on_vulnerability.)
3. When have you experienced a lack of our most basic human need—connection—in your life?

Again, reflect on these questions, and allow yourself to be wrong and to be open to new perspectives. By doing so, you'll likely find new insights in the most unexpected places.

5

GROW YOUR COLLECTION OF "USED-TO-THINKS"

If you judge people, you have no time to love them.
—Mother Teresa

Tell me about your collection of "used-to-thinks." You know what I mean—"I used to think that _____, but now I don't." Or "I used to think every _____ got _____, but now I see it the other way." That's a "used-to-think" (U2T).

The older I get, the bigger my collection of U2Ts becomes. In fact, my collection seems to be getting exponentially larger as I age. What about yours?

If you're like me, your U2T collection started growing somewhere in your late teens or early 20s. Prior to that age (again, if you were like me) I had nothing in my collection at all. This is because I was the typical (or maybe even a bit of an extreme example of a) full-time know-it-all when I was young. Some people might say "insufferable" would be a good adjective to describe me back then. What about you? Were you insufferable too? (Let's start a focus group—recovering, insufferable, full-time know-it-alls, or RIFTKIAs. Ha!)

I'm convinced one of the areas of serious and continuous conflict between parents and their insufferable, full-time know-it-all children, and be-tween managers and their "problem employees," is one of "used-to-think dissonance." (**OK**, the psy-chologists in the world are cringing—but I like this term I just invented. I'm going to keep using it!) When we haven't developed enough U2Ts, we tend to operate with a limited perspective that's charac-terized by our "need to be right." Unfortunately, rather than remembering (and honoring) the pro-cess by which we as parents and/or managers have acquired our U2Ts (trial and error, mistakes, epiph-anies, etc.), we try to *prove* to our kids or employees that they don't know it all.

So, how does the need to prove we are right work for us? It's often like having "nitro" meet "glycerin." *Boom!*

Within the past few years, I have added a *big* U2T to my collection: I used to think that achiev-ing balance was the key to a successful, happy life. Now I know that's not true. This was a hard-fought lesson, and my learning went this way: The more I strove to find balance, the more elusive it be-came. It was as if I was trying to hold smoke in my hands—each time I "thought" I'd achieved balance, the scale would tip the other way, and I'd be back out of balance. Further, it didn't matter what I was trying to balance. Work and family. Employee satisfaction and a strong bottom line. Weekend getaways and home repair. My work as an author, a speaker, and a consultant. Whatever I was trying to keep in balance just kept shifting out of balance.

It was frustrating. And as I learned later, pointless.

Why is it pointless? Because balance *never* happens, at least for long. You may be in balance for that split second when the scales go in opposite directions, but that's it. And trying to "stay" in balance means you're constantly trading-off one thing (e.g., employee satisfaction) for something else (profit). Trade-offs represent "lose—lose," or "win—lose" thinking, and that's just not a powerful way to operate in the long term.

Instead, making choices by *being centered in principles* means there's no need to try to balance anything. They might be principles such as "I'd rather be joyful than try to prove to anyone that I'm right" or "I will be the change I want to see in the world" or "I choose to be an indispensable member of my team" or "I choose to be responsible and effective related to driving profit so I'm able to do the volunteer work that I love." As a result, the typical "I can't keep things in balance" symptoms like frustration, resentment, and anger just disappear.

And—we can relax (deep cleansing breath).

So, to summarize, here's my new thought to replace my U2T: Balance (looking for trade-offs) is not the answer—being centered (grounding my choices in meaningful principles) is the answer. Let me say it again, balance is not the answer—being centered is the answer.

Here's an example from my personal life related to the difference between "balance" and "centeredness." I've been asked this question before:

"Bob—you have four children. Do you love them equally?" Pause. (How would *you* answer this question?)

Here's my answer—no. I don't love my children equally (balanced); I love them uniquely (centered). There's no scorekeeping, debits-equaling-credits, calendar-management stuff going on—I am simply centered in my approach that I will be the father each of my children needs me to be. By making that decision, I love them the way *they need me* to love them, not the way I think I *should* love them.

That's centeredness. And that's one of my converted "used-to-thinks."

How big is your collection of U2Ts? If you're like me, aren't you amazed at how much less you "know" as you get older? I am. And I realize that *all* of my converted U2Ts are gifts that came along with experience, with newfound wisdom, with more trips around the sun, etc. I can't wait to add another converted U2T today. How about you?

Questions, Insights, Implications

1. What does the distinction between "balance" and "centeredness" mean to you?
2. What are your most profound "used-to-thinks"—and what was involved in your process of discovering them?
3. What might happen if you were willing to

reconsider something that you absolutely believe is true—even for a moment?

Again, reflect on these questions, and allow yourself to be wrong and to be open to new perspectives. By doing so, you'll likely find new insights in the most unexpected places.

6

THE HIGH COST OF
AVOIDING CONFLICT

Employees waste an average of $1,500 and an
8-hour workday for every crucial conversation they
avoid. These costs skyrocket when multiplied by the
prevalence of conflict avoidance. And, 95 percent
of a company's workforce struggles to speak up to
their colleagues about their concerns. As a result,
they engage in resource-sapping avoidance tactics
including ruminating excessively about crucial issues,
complaining, getting angry, doing unnecessary work
and avoiding the other person altogether.

—Joseph Grenny, *Crucial Conversations*

Getting to "what's right" often involves deep disagreement and significant conflict. However, for far too many of us, we'd rather get a root canal or have our gums scraped than actively seek out conflict. And we're wrong about that.

It's time to fix our perspectives about conflict.

Conflict is a needed element in driving for and achieving the best possible outcomes among people. The absence of conflict is a terrifying thing—described accurately by the term "group think"—where no one is actually questioning the validity, currency, depth, relevance, or appropriateness of decisions and directions. It's the equivalent of creating "zombie-like" agreement, where no one steps forward to say the "emperor has no clothes."

We need differences of opinion. We need alternative viewpoints. We need disagreement—as long as all of it is focused on making things better, faster, cheaper, or more beneficial. However, conflict can quickly become unproductive in one of two ways:

1. One is when we fall into the trap of "being triggered"—when our fight-or-flight needs

rush forward (because we feel threatened) or when historic situations have far too much influence over our present-moment interactions (so that we use automatic responses). This is what I call "autopilot-based, unproductive conflict." (I'll talk more about this in a bit.)

2. Another is when we consciously avoid it. Some of us will spend hours, days, weeks, or even longer avoiding conflict that could actually provide value. As a result, we create passively unproductive conflict by keeping the hard conversations in the shadows.

Now, some personality types (extreme introverts, for example) will have more difficulty in stopping their conflict-avoiding behaviors. However, regardless of where you are on the conflict spectrum (Evel Knievel on one end, and the *very* conflict-avoiding person on the other), changing our relationship to conflict is helpful. Think of conflict as a necessary ingredient in great outcomes. After all, how does one make scrambled eggs? By exerting active, intentional conflict on the eggs—that's how.

I actually had someone ask me once, "Why do you ever talk to that person? All they seem to do is disagree with you!" I thought to myself: "I'm counting on that! I look forward to the conversation!" Then again, I know I may not represent the typical person in that I will normally run straight toward disagreement and on purpose! I've come to rely on conflict as a tool. It's something that helps to create extraordinary outcomes. It can be the same for you too.

Next, let's address the other big secret related to the other kind of unproductive conflict: when we're triggered, either by feelings of being threatened or when our automatic, conditioned responses take over.

Triggers come in a variety of forms. A trigger could be seeing a particular person's face; smelling something attached to one of our memories; receiving an email, phone call, or text from a specific source; or seeing a meeting notice pop up. Really, it can be virtually any type of stimulus. And then—if it is truly a trigger—our autopilot presents us with a conditioned response. It could be fear, anger, anxiety, or tension, but rarely is it a positive response. Many such triggers get ensnared into our relationships—especially relationships involving strong feelings like those between spouses and between parents and children.

Here's an example—teenagers, especially young teens—can be particularly prone to acting like triggers. Any triggers coming to mind here? Anybody find teenagers difficult? Challenging? Frustrating? Alas, all of those feelings are "learned." There's nothing inherently challenging about a teenager— if you put the potential conflict involved with raising that teenager in perspective.

The job of a teenager is to break free from his or her parents and to begin establishing a distinct identity. However, too few parents honor what their teenage kids are doing, and as a result, these parents actually work to drive unproductive conflict. We create buttons for one another—guilt buttons, shame buttons, sarcasm buttons, anger buttons— and often, the closer the relationship, the more we feel empowered to push the button! And the responses to the buttons get hardwired into our minds—like a light switch. Flip the switch, and on goes the light. Trigger a teenager (through sarcasm, belittling, shaming, anger, etc.), and you create unproductive conflict.

That is, until you do something to interrupt the circuit.

If someone pushes our buttons, we have the opportunity to do something other than react. We can wait—about one-half a second is all it takes. That's the length of time for any stimulus to go all the way through the prefrontal cortex to bring in all of the executive decision-making functions that allow a person to take different paths. We can stop the automatic response.

As to our teenagers, in that one-half second, we can remind ourselves of just how crappy our own teenage years might have been and how frustrated we got when our parents "pushed" our buttons. Maybe, just maybe, in that short interruption between stimulus and response, we might find a bit of compassion, understanding, and patience. And it turns out that's most likely the *exact* thing our teenagers are seeking! Boom. No more unproductive conflict.

It's just a matter of inserting that extra half a second between stimulus and response. Try it. Try it here just for a moment. The next time you see a highly charged Facebook post, news story, Tweet, or whatever—with a viewpoint you vehemently disagree with—give yourself a half a second, get out of your emotional alligator brain for a moment, and then let it go through a different path.

You may choose to have no response. I have to tell you that's a healthier and happier place to be sometimes. Or you may allow yourself to do some creative problem-solving—and look for a better approach than using your conditioned responses. In any case, you're giving yourself the time (again, half a second) to explore other options. That's a *very* good thing.

Five Steps to Stop Unproductive Conflict Before It Starts

1. Step off the curb and address potential conflicts as they come forward—don't wait, and

certainly don't ruminate.

2. If you find yourself trapped in conflict-avoiding behavior, change your self-talk about it. Give yourself permission to view conflict as a productivity-enhancing thing. Conflict is a tool to help us get better.

3. Practice higher levels of awareness when it comes to being triggered. In other words, recognize (even after the fact) that you've been triggered, and you are about to do, or are in the midst of doing, or have just done what you've always done.

4. Treat yourself with compassion when you are unsuccessful in handling conflict immediately and/or when you allow yourself to be triggered into unproductive conflict.

5. Begin to predict your potential responses—either conflict avoidance or being triggered—as you plan your day, week, etc. If a situation with someone is likely to create fears of conflict or create the possibility of a trigger, coach yourself through making a plan ahead of time.

Remember—our feeling about and our responses to conflict are totally up to us to manage. No one, repeat, no one has the power to make us feel anything without our permission.

Questions, Insights, Implications

1. How would you describe your relationship with conflict? Do you do everything you can to avoid it? Do you understand its value? Do you create it intentionally? What might be different for you if you had a different relationship with conflict?

2. What are your triggers—things that bring about conditioned responses? What situations (people, places, events, etc.) are most likely to trigger you?

3. Have you considered the role you play in triggering others (children, spouses, employees, neighbors, etc.)? What if you were more intentional in your approach to communication—and honored your desire to stop triggering others?

Again, reflect on these questions, and allow yourself to be wrong and to be open to new perspectives. By doing so, you'll likely find new insights in the most unexpected places.

7

BE KIND—
EVERYONE HAS A STORY

Life is short and we have never too much time for
gladdening the hearts of those who are travelling the
dark journey with us. Oh be swift to love,
make haste to be kind.
—Henri Frédéric Amiel

Everyone who is reading this is struggling with something—right now. Everybody. No question, rather than admit we're struggling, we often prefer to put ourselves in our fancy cars and big houses while sporting new clothes, great haircuts, and perfect makeup (as I shared in a previous chapter). It's more comfortable to go through the world and put our public persona out for display. However, every now and then, we let our guard down and let the challenges behind our masks be visible.

Imagine seeing somebody stuck at a stoplight, just not moving. What's your immediate reaction? Mine? I tend to jump to the conclusion that the person is on a smartphone texting, reading Facebook, or something else like that. However, maybe I could consider the fact that the person may have just gotten some bad news and is sitting there trying to deal with it and being distracted as a result. What happens if that person cuts in front of you in traffic or someone doesn't return a phone call or an email? We have ready-made stories for their behavior too, right?

Maybe there's a 100 percent-opposite approach

we could take. What do you think? Maybe we could offer a moment of compassion, tell ourselves that maybe there's a different perspective. What if—instead of going negative—we could choose to assume best intentions as opposed to saying to ourselves, "They just blew me off!"

Again, everybody is struggling with something. To turn the topic around just a little bit, when somebody's struggling, the right response is not to jump into the middle of that person's suffering, to commiserate and deal with it, or worse yet, to try to solve it. The hard lesson I've learned through my life as I've gotten older is that I can't take on someone's suffering for him or her. I can't. What I can do instead is I can empathize with where that person is.

I have a friend whose wife suffers from severe, often-debilitating depression. He told me once that he, personally, had stopped her in the middle of suicide attempts—twice. She's struggled with medications, with therapy, with *every* approach known to the human race to manage her depression. My friend told me that well-meaning people often have no idea what to do. They offer words of encouragement ("You can do it!"), they offer help and support ("If you *ever* need anything, just ask."), and they offer attempts at understanding ("My _____ also suffers from depression and has found that _____ works.") My friend told me that each of these approaches actually makes his wife feel worse, not better. I asked him, "So, what is one thing that someone has offered, or something a person has done, that actually made a difference?" He asked his wife, and she responded, "There's one person who comes over, sits on the couch with me, and just rubs my feet. No words, no encouragement, no pity—just the simple act of rubbing my feet."

Who, among all the people who have been in your life, gave you the most comfort when you were at the deepest, darkest spot in your life? Maybe it was the person who came over, sat on the couch, and did nothing but rub your feet. The person didn't say anything or offer problem-solving or advice. That person just sat with you, in your darkness, and rubbed your feet.

I'm going to invite you to think about that

coworker who annoys you or that person down the street who drives you crazy or the neighbor upstairs who won't be quiet—anybody who has something about him or her that bothers you. And just today, just once, instead of judging and belittling and shaming, ask what's that person's story? What is he or she struggling with today? By being more empathetic with others, with taking a moment to see what life is like from their side of the table, our need to be right about things tends to melt away.

Remember—we're all suffering with something. Be kind. Especially to yourself.

Questions, Insights, Implications

1. What might change in your daily life when you have the awareness that each person is struggling with some form of suffering?

2. Are there times and places where a simple act of compassion and empathy (the act of just rubbing someone's feet) has profoundly affected you?

3. Stop, take a moment, and consider someone else's story. What insights can you draw from the past that are related to someone's reaction in a situation?

Again, reflect on these questions, and allow yourself to be wrong and to be open to new perspectives. By doing so, you'll likely find new insights in the most unexpected places.

8

HUMANIZING "THE OTHER"

If you ask what percentage of your genes is reflected
in your external appearance, the basis by which we
talk about race, the answer is in the range
of .01 percent. This is a very, very minimal
reflection of your genetic makeup.
—Dr. Harold P. Freeman
(chief executive, president, and director of surgery
at North General Hospital in Manhattan)

Human beings are great at categorizing and arranging—this goes here; that goes there. We do that with our stuff, *and* we do that with the people in our lives. Separating, in and of itself, isn't the problem. (After all, red M&Ms are just as tasty as green M&Ms!) It's when we attach value-based, good-versus-bad labels to different groups that we get ourselves into trouble. There's this camp and that camp, separated by attributes that are demographic, financial, racial, gender oriented, sexual orientation related, weight based, age based, political—you name it. And then we look at all the different boxes we've arranged and start to say, "My box is not only different from your box, but my box is *better* than your box." This behavior spells trouble. We spend so much time in our individual boxes—looking out at the other boxes—that we tend to start looking at the other boxes as being wrong. Different equals wrong somehow.

Taken to an extreme, we experience bigotry and hatred. All of this is learned behavior based upon biases we are shown—either directly or indirectly—throughout our lives. No one is born a racist, and according to Dr. Freeman, only about one one-hundredth of one percent (0.01 percent) of our DNA has anything to do with our appearance—including our skin color, the size and shape of our noses, and our hair type, ears, freckles, etc. Again, *no one* is born a racist. It's a learned behavior. And if something like racism is learned, it can be unlearned. However, we need to take a first step to make that happen by starting to look at "what's right." For example, consider these assertions: 1. Life, liberty, and the pursuit of happiness are unalienable rights; and 2. All men [*sic*] are created equal. Both of these statements come from the United States Declaration of Independence, a document *many* claim as the measure of "what's right" but few truly *live*. Don't get me started on the Bible. Until we're ready to start looking at "what's right," we'll be stuck in justifying our bias by arguing "who's right."

If we're really going to start moving the world together in a way that we can get to focusing on what the world needs, which is some healing and some sensibility and some open dialogue, the first thing we need to do is to humanize "the other," those who live in that "other" box.

Here's an example of what I do when it comes to humanizing others. I've been conducting a research project about understanding how people look at everyday activities such as driving, commuting, eating, traveling, and such. I'm using the #helpmeunderstand hashtag. I have a very diverse set of friends on Facebook, and two of them are diametrically opposed in their political and religious views. They couldn't be more different—on the surface. One is a conservative Jew, and the other is a proud Muslim. One is male; the other is female.

That said, on the same post (it was about our views of personal body space in public settings), one right after the other, they commented on what it's like to ride the subway in New York City. They both described how much they disliked the experience, and their comments mirrored each other almost 100 percent. As I read their thoughts, I thought to myself, "In another context, they may not give themselves permission to actually speak to each other—at all! However, when referring to an everyday, mundane, ordinary situation—this notion of sitting on a subway in New York—they were able to humanize each other and share something in common. They didn't look at their profile pictures; they didn't look at their "about me" sections on their Facebook profiles. They just simply commented on what was in front of them.

Again, only about 0.01 percent of human DNA has anything to do with our appearance. It amazes me how much *baggage* we have as a species about appearance and how much physical visual cues separate us. How about we spend more time looking toward connection, by recognizing the humanity (the other 99.99 percent) in those around us. Once we're able to see the human in those in "the other" group, we'll no longer be able to dismiss them. We can take a step forward in their direction.

Questions, Insights, Implications

1. Have you ever considered—by relative percentage—the tiny percentage of our DNA that is related to appearance? What does this insight trigger for you?

2. How do you feel about the idea that we innately and unconsciously separate and categorize when it comes to "other" people?

3. Are there other examples in which you've seen yourself or others around you humanizing "the other" through shared experiences (as in the story about the New York subway above)?

Again, reflect on these questions, and allow yourself to be wrong and to be open to new perspectives. By doing so, you'll likely find new insights in the most unexpected places.

9

WHAT ENERGY ARE
YOU BRINGING?

While you're going through this process of trying
to find the satisfaction in your work, pretend you
feel satisfied. Tell yourself you had a good day. Walk
through the corridors with a smile rather than a
scowl. Your positive energy will radiate. If you act
like you're having fun, you'll find you are having fun.
—Jean Chatzky

There's an old saying: "Check yourself before you wreck yourself." I'd like to amend the saying: "Check the energy you're bringing to a situation before you wreck the meeting, the birthday party, or the conversation with your family."

What energy are you bringing?

I'll give you an example. I remember a conversation with a coworker years ago that went something like this:

Coworker: "Man, I'm really not looking forward to *that* meeting."

Me: "Why?"

Coworker: "Well, you know, that person— they're *so* negative. They disagree with everything all the time. I'm sick of it."

Me: "Oh, I look forward to disagreement. I'm excited about the meeting!"

Coworker (wearing stunned expression): "Are you nuts?"

Me: "I love having people disagree with me. It's a chance to find a better answer." The coworker rolls his eyes, gives me the "you're freaking crazy" look, and walks away muttering while shaking his head.

The point is this: Both my coworker and I had a choice about the energy we were going to bring to the meeting. I was excited and anticipating the meeting while my coworker was already suffering in advance. He'd convinced himself the meeting was going to be hard and needed to be endured rather than be something to look forward to. What do you do typically? Think about the number of meetings that you have on a daily basis and how many of them you go to with an excited or anticipatory energy as opposed to an attitude of "ugh, not another meeting."

By the way, here's the *big* secret about our energy: The energy we send is the energy we receive. If you're displaying confrontational, angry, pissed-off energy, guess what the universe will send right back your way? Yep. Those around you will seem confrontational, angry, and pissed off. On the other hand, if you send curious, patient, inclusive, and collaborative energy, the universe will reflect that back to you. *Our* energy is completely under our control—*every* time. Martin Luther King Jr. knew that, even in the face of unbelievable negativity, he was still able to choose his own emotion. In other words, maybe you just had a hard conversation at home, or traffic was horrible, or you got a flat tire on your way to work. Maybe you should leave the resulting emotions tied to the flat tire where they belong, in the trunk with the flat, as opposed to dragging them upstairs into your office. Just let them be.

Here's another place where our energy management is so critical: learning something new or taking on a new role or a new project. What comes to mind when I say, "Let's learn a new language!" We're going to use Rosetta Stone, and we're going to learn Chinese, Spanish, or French. Do you bring curiosity? Do you think about it as an interesting challenge? Or do you start talking to yourself this way: "I can't do this. I don't want to sound like a nine-month-old when I'm speaking this new language. I don't want to sound like an idiot!"

The "I can't do this" is the energy of censorship and fear. It's back to the "suffering in advance" my coworker demonstrated about the meeting. Instead, think about bringing the energy of discovery, a beginner's mentality that says I'm willing to stumble when it comes to something new. Until we're able to be willing to be vulnerable enough with ourselves to risk looking foolish or to endure potential criticism about our struggles to speak Spanish, we're unlikely to move very far toward "what's right." We're still going to be stuck in "who's right" (ourselves, in this case).

The last area I want to address about our energy is this one: The energy related to our choices is *critical.* Our lives don't so much revolve around what happens to us; our lives are *much* more influenced by the choices we make. Here's an example. (And yes, it's a religious story, but it's a good story because there's a surprising twist in it.)

I'm pretty confident we've all heard the story of the Good Samaritan, but we've trivialized it so much over the years that the *power* of the story has been lost. Back in first-century Judea, to the Jewish people there was *no such thing* as a good Samaritan. In fact, the Samaritans were looked at with such derision and such negativity that today you could take whatever group that's completely on the other side of your belief system, and that would be the equivalent of a Samaritan. (KKK? Isis? Yep—insert one of *those* groups into your thought process, and you'll get the idea of the Jewish feelings toward Samaritans.)

Here's where the challenge of the story hits home. The injured traveler was ignored by two travelers, a priest and a Levite. On the other hand, the enemy, the outcast, the "other," the real negative, the member of the KKK, the Isis fighter—you choose—is the one who picked the person up, took him to an inn, took care of him, and paid in advance for his stay and care by the host at the inn. That's the power of that story; it's incredibly provocative. What choices do we make? What's the energy in them? How many times do we just "walk by" someone instead of bringing the energy of compassion? We don't understand the real purpose behind the Good Samaritan story anymore because it has just become a brand. We've got charities with the name Good Samaritan.

Let me invite you to think about the energy that you bring to a setting because you're going to get it back. Be curious. Be open. Be positive. Be anticipatory. Things will change in a significant way for you. I promise.

Questions, Insights, Implications

1. How good are you at choosing the energy you bring into a situation? If it's easy, why? If it's difficult, how come?

2. Are you naturally able to take on a "beginner's mind" when you start to learn something new? Or do your biases and conditioned ways of thinking get in the way?

3. How does the provocative description of the Good Samaritan story make you feel? How likely is it that we might experience a version of that story today?

Again, reflect on these questions, and allow yourself to be wrong and to be open to new perspectives. By doing so, you'll likely find new insights in the most unexpected places.

10

FOCUS ON INTERESTS, NOT POSITIONS

People listen better if they feel that you have understood them. They tend to think that those who understand them are intelligent and sympathetic people whose own opinions may be worth listening to. So if you want the other side to appreciate your interests, begin by demonstrating that you appreciate theirs.

—Roger Fisher, *Getting to Yes*

We seem to have a societal sickness these days. We don't seem to have any room available to appreciate someone else's interest. Instead, when people find themselves in a decision-making setting with a group of other people, they walk in with their body armor on, sit down at their seats, and fire up their force-field generators. Then they try to make a decision. Unfortunately, the walls that are up in front of them, coupled with the fact that they're dug in because they have a certain position they need to defend, means we often get nowhere in terms of making decisions.

Here's an example: Our political "system" has devolved into a mechanism of *perfecting* the "who's right" dysfunction because it is virtually 100 percent related to defending positions rather than appreciating interests. How about we turn it upside down and start thinking about it a little bit differently? What if we started with questions like these: "What are *we* really focusing on here? What are *we* really interested in? Where are *our* common interests?" When we look at interests instead of positions, we start to discover that *all* people are concerned about safety, want predictability, are fearful about change, and thirst to be included, to be appreciated, and to have a genuine sense of belonging.

When we start with either-or thinking, we push people into defensiveness, and we begin to see "it's my way or the highway" behaviors. We get stuck in binary choices—it's this way, or it's that way—that offer no in-between. We foster division and create (or accelerate) pain and anguish for people. What about creating "both-and" solutions? What about looking through the lens of "our common interests" instead of "I win; you lose" approaches?

Here's an example of what I'm talking about. I volunteer for an organization called Building Bridges. Its mission is focused clearly on shifting the conversation around one of the most challenging and seemingly intractable issues anywhere on Earth: the historic conflict between Israel and Palestine. This group brings groups of high school girls together (Palestinians, Israelis, and Americans; Jews, Muslims, and Christians) for a two-year intensive program designed to change the conversation. It's not about "normalizing" or "peacemaking";

instead, it's about finding common ground, about driving the realization that the interests of teenage girls are *far* more common than uncommon. One of the first exercises these girls participate in—and remember, there are some *deep* divisions between and among the demographic categories here—is to put their fingers on one another's carotid arteries. To feel one another's heartbeat. To *feel* the humanity in "the other." As the program progresses, the girls are invited to continue to deepen their understanding of what unites them (dating, body image, a sense of belonging, owning their femininity) as they deepen their appreciation of one another's individual situations. Words fail me in describing the *power* of this process. Let's just say the girls who participate, one person at a time, one family at a time, one street at a time, are beginning to shift the conversation toward "what's right" and away from "who's right."

When we are genuine in our desire for "what's right, not who's right" and are authentically looking for a way to end the world's madness, we start looking at interests and not positions. We aren't defending turf; we're seeking solutions. When teams and organizations operate from this viewpoint, decisions improve, decisions last longer, decisions are easier and *faster* to implement, and satisfaction grows.

Doesn't that sound like a great formula? Let's build some bridges.

Questions, Insights, Implications

1. Describe a situation where you've found yourself in the midst of conflict because someone is defending a position as opposed to searching for deeper interests.

2. What has led up to our society's preference to *not* look for "both-and" answers and instead move toward "either-or" thinking?

3. What comes to mind when you consider the Building Bridges approach to get teenage girls to experience the heartbeat in one another?

Again, reflect on these questions, and allow yourself to be wrong and to be open to new perspectives. By doing so, you'll likely find new insights in the most unexpected places.

11

KEEPING "WHAT'S RIGHT," IN FRONT

————————————

Although the world is full of suffering,
it is also full of the overcoming of it.
—Helen Keller

The challenge of getting to "what's right," which I've shared throughout this book, can be large. But I believe it's worth it. There's value in it, and I want to remind you about some steps to make it happen and to keep it in the forefront of your thinking and behaving.

First, let's remember the whole notion of "what's right, not who's right" is by definition countercultural. It's not something that we're used to doing, because when things get hard, or somebody disagrees with us, or we get pushback or outright conflict about something, most of us want to retreat. We either get very quiet and do nothing because we don't like conflict and we just want it to go away, or we become passive-aggressive and start conducting corrosive conversations by email or in a hallway after a meeting. We either start picking on one another, or we just crumble. We fall back. We feel we have no platform anymore.

Therefore, keeping "what's right" in front is something that's necessary to keep the energy moving, to keep us and the organizations we're part of going in the right direction. To keep it in front, let's bring back some of the big themes I shared with you earlier.

First, you need to check what energy you're bringing. Often, the leader is the source of the problem, not the source of the benefit. We have a client right now, and one of the leaders just keeps bringing up this negative incident from about a year ago. No matter how many times we invite this person to stop doing that, the person keeps mentioning it as an example of why the organization isn't changing. It may sound obvious to you as I write this, but every time this person brings up the incident, it just gives it more life. The incident continues to live on; in fact, it's become somewhat of a fish story! The incident was a problem, yes, but it wasn't the *huge* issue it had become in this person's mind.

My simple advice? *Stop it.* Don't give it more life. Don't bring that energy. Bring the energy of looking forward instead.

Next, be humble and vulnerable. This is something that's really challenging when you're looking at what's right. It took me a long time—until I was in my midthirties—before I recognized that asking for help is a sign of strength, not a sign of weakness. In fact, it's ultimately just really practical to ask for help. Why would you wander around just doing the wrong thing for a long period of time? Get some help. That requires a little bit of humility. It's the need to look at yourself and say maybe you don't have all the answers. Then when you find yourself in new situations, don't pretend like you know the answers. Act like a beginner. Be curious. Have all the information flow to you. Know-it-alls (And you know who you are!) are like balloons that are full of air. A full balloon can take on no more air. It'll pop. You've got to leave some room in your balloon to get some air in there, and that's a great metaphor for being open to learning, to discovering that maybe you don't know everything.

Then get your accountability equation right. Too often—in fact, *way* too often—I hear people say, "We need to hold them accountable." You've probably said it yourself more than once, maybe even today. To me, this statement is backward. Accountability isn't a demand or an external force I can force on someone else. It's an intrinsic, internal, personal choice. In other words, I can *be* accountable or not, but no one can *make me* be accountable. Does that make sense? When we're keeping "what's right" in front, we're acting from a place of personal accountability, and we're inviting others to do the same. Stop trying to hold someone accountable (by the way, this really should translate into "I want to punish you if you don't deliver") and, instead, invite that person to be accountable. This causes a major shift in the energy between people.

The last thing I want to bring up here is a really simple thing when it comes to keeping "what's right" in front. Eliminate your distractions. Quit checking your email, texting, Facebooking, Snapchatting, Instagramming, or whatever it might be that distracts you when you're with other people. Quit it! Give the people you're with the purity of your attention. There's no greater gift that we can give to another person than the purity of our attention. When that person knows that you're paying complete attention to him or her, that everything being said is being absorbed by you, everything changes.

While it's not easy keeping "what's right" in front, keeping this checklist in front of you can help:

- Check your energy.
- Be humble.
- Be vulnerable.
- Ask for help.
- Retain a beginner's mind.
- Be accountable, and invite others to do the same.
- Give the purity of your attention to others.

Questions, Insights, Implications

1. When you're in the midst of a challenging situation, what might happen if you were able to check the energy you're bringing and shift your energy to a more productive place?

2. What's your reaction when you think of the words "humble" and "vulnerable"?

3. Are you able to regularly give of the purity of your attention to others, or are you more frequently distracted by something (such as emails, texts, Facebook postings, eavesdropping)?

Again, reflect on these questions, and allow yourself to be wrong and to be open to new perspectives. By doing so, you'll likely find new insights in the most unexpected places.

12

DOES THIS "SHIFT" ACTUALLY WORK?

———————————

When we quit thinking primarily about ourselves
and our own self-preservation, we undergo a truly
heroic transformation of consciousness.
—Joseph Campbell

O ur history as human beings is littered with things about which we have been wrong. Epically wrong in many cases. Yes, I know there are still some "flat-Earth truthers" out there (a famous NBA player among them), but our historical viewpoint about the Earth's role in the larger universe has only been "right" for the briefest period of our existence. If you think of "conscious-humanness" as existing for maybe a hundred thousand years, we've known the Earth goes around the sun (not the reverse, or other nonsense about the structure of the universe) for about one half of one percent (0.5 percent) of our history. For the rest of the time, we had a number of theories that science ultimately disproved (the firmament holding back the "waters" of the universe is one of my favorites). In the following passage, Nancy Ellen Abrams, in her ambitious 2015 book titled *A God That Could Be Real,* discusses the past five hundred years or so as we learned the Earth isn't flat:

> Europeans living through this epic shift found it wrenching, almost impossible to

take in. The notion that the whole earth was moving simply defied common sense. The sixteenth-century philosopher Jean Bodin wrote, "No one in his senses, or imbued with the slightest knowledge of physics, will ever think that the earth, heavy and unwieldy from its own weight and mass, staggers up and down around its own center and that of the sun; for at the slightest jar of the earth, we would see cities and fortresses, towns and mountains thrown down." Martin Luther wrote: "People gave ear to an upstart astrologer who strove to show that the earth revolves, not the heavens or the firmament, the sun and the moon. . . . This fool wishes to reverse the entire science of astronomy, but sacred Scripture tells us that Joshua commanded the sun to stand still, and not the earth." The new scientific picture of the solar system flouted both common sense and religious authority. But it won out because it worked: its predictions were in perfect agreement with observations of tides, eclipses, and the motions of comets, asteroids, the planets, and their moons. The new physics was so empowering that enthusiastic adopters extrapolated its applicability to the entire universe.

Far from the example of literally shifting one's world view to the planet being round and revolving around the sun as the sun moved in the galaxy—as cited in the quote above—here's an example from modern-day life that illustrates the power of changing attitudes from "who's right" to "what's right."

This is a true story about one of my clients.

The nearly one hundred attendees had arranged themselves in "pods" separated by the color and logo on their shirts. It reminded me of a middle school dance—except these were adults, coworkers. The large meeting room was eerily quiet as the workers flipped through the information packet given to them as they came in the room. Aside from the occasional muted snicker and some scattered coughs and sneezes, no conversation was taking place. The air conditioning system was abnormally amplified in the absence of human-based sound.

The tension was palpable. So was the mistrust, the fear, the skepticism, and the anger. Few people in the room demonstrated any positive emotion. They clearly didn't want to be there, and they couldn't wait to be away from "the others" in the room.

And then I stood up to address the group.

I was prepared. I'd done my homework. I knew the dynamics in the room. A report from the finance department—based upon superficial and, in some cases, flawed research—indicated the group could save $1 million a year for five years. All that was needed was the termination of eighteen staff members and a massive, bureaucratic, "jam-it-down-their-throats" approach to making organizational changes. Flawed or not, the report had gotten the attention of senior executives, and the expectations to save money—or else—were very clear.

However, the two senior leaders representing the group assembled before me were aware of the "Design the Future Process" my team and I had developed over the years. They knew the power of creating change *through* people, rather than doing change *to* people, because I'd helped them before. They had asked the senior executives to give them a chance to do something different, and they were given six months—or else. At that point, they asked me to get involved and see whether the group would be open to a new approach to choosing and implementing a new future. I agreed.

That day was the first meeting of the entire group.

I cleared my throat, looked around the room, and began: "Thank you for coming. I have an invitation for you—one that I'll challenge you to accept, but one that I won't force on you. I'm aware of the finance department report, and I know how you feel about it."

I waited. I felt the anger and skepticism in the room.

I continued, "Are you open to being proactive, to being accountable, to examining a new future, to taking a stance about what will work best for you? Are you up for doing something completely different—where *you* will be creating the recommendations, not the finance department?"

Silence. Crossed arms. Heads cocked. Bored faces, rolling eyes, sneers.

I went on, "Like I said, it's an invitation. Your executives are giving you the chance to do the right thing—to focus on 'what's right for your organization' and not on 'who's right in the head office.' Are you up for that?"

No breakthrough happened during the first meeting, but I didn't expect one to. However, the energy shifted from "who cares" to "maybe there's something here." A crack was all I wanted.

Now, suffice it to say, through a facilitated process over the next several weeks and months, this group made great choices. Its members eventually recommended changes, based upon "what's right, not who's right," that resulted in not just saving $5 million over five years but more than *three times* that amount. *And* all eighteen people got to keep their jobs.

I still remember the final celebration with them. It looked and felt 100 percent different from their first meeting. There was no division based upon "logos and colors"; everyone sat with everyone. There was laughing, teasing, clapping, cheering, pats on the back, hugs, and even some tears. It was joyous, boisterous, exciting, and wonderful. They celebrated their success—together.

What did they do differently in the process they used? They came together, they built trust, they shared their great ideas, and they listened—all based upon doing what's right. Oh—I haven't yet mentioned this—what was the group? They were the public works, police, and fire fleets in the city and county of Denver, and the project was called the Fleet Analysis and Optimization Project. (See the case study here: www.teamtipton.com/portfolio_page/city-and-county-of-denver-fleet-optimization.)

The results they created don't sound much like government, do they? If a governmental organization can do this, so can *any* other organization in *any* other industry. So can yours.

Questions, Insights, Implications

1. Have you found yourself in a truly toxic, dysfunctional situation (at home or at work)? What was your response?

2. How do you feel about the notion that shifting worldviews starts with us, individually? Are you the type who says, "As soon as you're done changing, everything will be fine"?

3. How open are you to the possibility that truly remarkable outcomes are possible even in the face of "evidence" that tells you it's impossible?

Again, reflect on these questions, and allow yourself to be wrong and to be open to new perspectives. By doing so, you'll likely find new insights in the most unexpected places.

13

Let's Heal the World—
an Open Invitation

Heal the world, make it a better place, for you and
for me, and the entire human race, there are people
dying, if you care enough for the living, make a
better place, for you and for me.
—Michael Jackson

What a big topic. Wow! Healing the world. Sure, Bob, let's heal the world. How do you suggest we get started doing that? I have an answer. Let's start small—very small, actually. If we want to play a role in healing the world, we have to heal ourselves first. We need to be able to own our own imperfections, we need to be able to own our vulnerabilities, and we need to be willing to see ourselves objectively and have a relationship with ourselves in which we can heal who we are.

Think about this for a second. Suppose you had an opportunity to go back and talk to the ten-year-old you. What would you tell the ten-year-old you that you've learned over the last—whatever it might be—twenty, thirty, or forty years? What kind of conversation would you have? My ten-year-old me was, well, somewhat tragic in many ways. I was tall, *really* skinny, had buckteeth, was getting some acne—and was a straight A student too, by the way. I also was a very serious kid. There were things that had to be examined, discussed, analyzed. I worried about everything! Now, given this picture of my ten-year-old self, let's just say members of the opposite sex weren't really "into" Bob back then (grin).

I used to be pretty hard on myself. You too? Many, many of us have been hard on ourselves for much of our lives. Again, what might you share with your ten-year-old self? I've done that, and here's what I said: "Relax. It all turns out fine. It gets better. The world isn't this place that you think it is right now. No need to be perfect; in fact, you're going to lose out on a lot of joy in your life because you will try for perfection. It's not possible, so just relax about it." One of life's biggest and hardest-fought lessons for me was giving myself permission to be OK with my imperfections. And once I was able to do that with and for myself, I was able to see that others were imperfect. I discovered I could love others through their imperfections, just as I hoped they would love me through mine. Don't be shocked by imperfection—the world is full of it! Each of us is imperfect in a beautiful way.

Another critical piece of "healing the world" involves recognizing the fact that how we do anything is how we do everything, especially when it comes to interacting with and treating people. The

way people treat their Uber driver will predict the
way they treat their children. I can tell a great deal
about people by the way they treat somebody from
whom they have nothing to gain—like their server
in a restaurant, a flight attendant, a hotel desk clerk,
a rental car agent. If they're dismissive, or if they
look down their nose, that tells me a lot about them.
To me, there isn't a situational nature about how
you deal with people. It's a cop-out to say, "It's just
business!" No, actually, kindness isn't situational —
nor is compassion, care, or courtesy. Want to heal
the world? Heal the way you interact with anyone.
It'll change the way you interact with everyone.

Then there's the last thing I want to talk about
related to healing the world. It starts with a four-letter word, and it ends with the same four-letter word.
This four-letter word? Love. Now, that may sound
strange to you. It may sound strange to others. But
I tell the people who work with me and for me that
I love them. I tell my clients that I love them. And
I demonstrate that in various ways. It's a process of
seeing through their imperfections, holding them in
a place where they're able to succeed, and being

able to look beyond this notion of me versus you, an either-or viewpoint. The viewpoint should be both-and, and there should be a focus on what's right, not who's right.

Let's heal the world, one person at a time. Start with yourself, and then take it one group, one team, one neighborhood, one family, one community, one business at a time as you expand out. What do you say? Are you up for it? It's my open invitation for you.

Questions, Insights, Implications

1. Are you someone who finds yourself disappointed or frustrated when faced with someone's imperfection (for example, bad service at a restaurant or an oversight by a coworker during a meeting)?

2. How do you feel about the notion that how you do anything is how you do everything? Can you "be" two different people in two different situations?

3. Do you believe that love is universal—in relationships (kids, spouse, friends), in business, in politics, with the environment—or is love something situational (it belongs here but not there)?

Again, reflect on these questions, and allow yourself to be wrong and to be open to new perspectives. By doing so, you'll likely find new insights in the most unexpected places.

EPILOGUE

No question, it takes courage (and patience) to look for "what's right" answers in a sea of "who's right" personalities. In my experience, leaders who are able to do this don't think less "of" themselves; they think less "about" themselves. They are able to quiet the needs of their ego as they focus on making connections instead of harping on the things that separate us. They align us around common interests instead of pushing us into defending positions. They look for similarities and bring positive energy to all situations.

I believe fervently in the *vast* goodness of humanity (a few aberrations aside) and seek to drive positive, powerful energy everywhere I go. Ultimately, I believe the only thing that matters is the people in our lives—our relationships—and treating others as we would like to be treated is a good starting point. However, seeing the individual humanity in one another means going another step forward—treating others as *they* would prefer to be treated. I've heard some call this approach the *Platinum Rule*.

Be the change you want to see. Get to "what's right." You can do it. I have confidence in you.

ABOUT THE AUTHOR

Bob Tipton is a high-energy, innovative, and insightful transformational-change architect, leadership facilitator, keynote speaker, and author who is passionate about helping individuals, groups, and entire organizations reach for and achieve exceptional results. While it seems the need for transformational change exists everywhere, he specializes in five primary areas: 1) government (local, state, federal); 2) utilities (water, wastewater, power, transportation); 3) education (K–12, higher ed); 4) health care (provider-based); and 5) nonprofits/foundations.

Organizations in these areas tend to be institutionalized and bureaucratic. Some may say they are among the most difficult in which to make change "really" happen. However, he disagrees. Each of these areas also shares a common bond: the desire to serve people. It's this "kernel" of serving the greater good that he works to reignite, to awaken from hibernation, to leverage in helping these organizations move toward greatness in what they do. Call him naive; call him delusional. It matters not. He *loves* to serve these kinds of organizations and help them remember the power and joy in what they do.

Bob is married to his high school sweetheart, and together they have four children and two grandchildren (thus far!). Living in the Denver area, he is a fourth-generation native of Colorado. He loves to travel and is a voracious, curious reader and a champion for causes involving children.

Reach out to Bob through his keynote speaker website: www.TiptonSpeaks.com.

APPENDIX

About Team Tipton

(What's right, not who's right in the world of work:
www.TeamTipton.com)

Far from being mumbo jumbo or "woo-woo," focusing on "what's right, not who's right" delivers profound benefits and results for organizations. You've read about one such example from our portfolio of work—the city and county of Denver—where an employee-led project turned up 300-plus percent more benefit than a top-down, in-your-face approach. Here's another example from a different client: Aurora Water's Prairie Waters Project (PWP)   (www.teamtipton.com/portfolio_page/ aurora-water-prairie-waters-project). The PWP was the project of the year in 2011 for both the American Public Works Association (APWA) and the Project Management Institute (PMI). Coming in on time, on schedule, on quality, and within risk parameters, the PWP saved the ratepayers for Aurora Water more than $100 million from the original project costs. Certainly there were a number of factors leading to the savings and the formal recognition of the PWP. However, *The Guide to Lean Enablers for Managing Engineering Programs*, which was conducted and published by the Joint MIT, PMI, INCOSE Community of Practice on Lean in Program Management* (www.teamtipton.com/wordpress/wp-content/uploads/2017/04/oehm-enetal2012-theguidetoleanenablersformanagingen-gineeringprograms.pdf), cited the PWP's culture of "what's right, not who's right" as being central to the excellence delivered by the PWP team. (On page 35, the *Guide* says, "The Prairie Waters program reports a culture of 'what's right' and not 'who's right,' emphasizing the fact that everybody's ideas are heard and treated equally, regardless of their position in the organization.")

It's simple, really. When you get a group of talented, skilled, committed professionals focusing on the big picture, a "what's right" vision, they'll come together and do great things. I see it *all* the time. All organizations are in a state of change. Whether navigating a senior leadership transition, refining a mission, improving products, launching a large-scale project, onboarding new employees, or responding to crises, organizations find there is always a change process under way. Yet while we are all familiar with the saying that "change is the only constant," very few organizations are equipped with the tools to navigate change smoothly and successfully.

Team Tipton is an extraordinary group of individuals, all of whom operate from the "what's right" viewpoint. We've come together to drive powerful transformational change and have developed three strategic imperatives for our work together:

Values: An organization either stands by its values, or it doesn't. There's no middle ground. At Team Tipton, we believe all great leaders want the best for their organizations, their employees, and their communities. We help our clients operate from a values-first perspective that drives cultures of high respect and high performance.

Vision: The research is pretty clear: Nothing motivates us more than working from our strengths. At Team Tipton, we believe that individuals reach their highest potential only if they are motivated by a compelling vision, are invited to contribute their best, and understand why their work matters. It's simple, really—a shared, powerful vision makes all the difference.

Velocity: The world isn't slowing down for anyone. At Team Tipton, we believe our clients need transformational, agile, and high-velocity approaches related to planning for the future, navigating uncertainty, overcoming obstacles, and transforming their workplaces. When this happens, spectacular results are everywhere.

For more than thirty years, I've been using the "what's right, not who's right" model to refine Team Tipton's innovative approach for guiding organizations through future-forward, results-focused transformational change initiatives. With a game-changing approach toward driving strategic growth and positive culture shifts, the Team Tipton model has been successful in sectors that include government agencies, public works, utilities, nonprofits, health care, and education.

We'd love to have the chance to work with you too.

BOOK CLUB GUIDE

Chapter 1

1. Describe a situation when you needed to just shut up and listen. No justifying, no pleading, no trying to convince someone that you were right—just a time your mouth needed to close, and your ears needed to open. How did you feel?

2. When have you felt a strong sense of accomplishment and pride as a result of you doing the right thing—even when it was extremely difficult?

3. What value might you see in offering to be contrite, vulnerable, and truly remorseful in a situation where you've wronged someone else?

Chapter 2

1. What evidence do you see that we have a worldwide epidemic of people needing to be right?

2. When have you seen challenges in your own life, community, and so on associated with "who's right" (wars, political infighting,

greed, family divisions, terrorism)?

3. Can you envision what the results might be of setting expectations through "agreements together" before meetings start? Before decisions are made?

Chapter 3

1. What are the causes behind our tendency to tend to render instant judgment without healthy curiosity?

2. What are your views about the acceptability of "alternative facts"?

3. Have you seen examples of the "ignorance, stupidity, evil progression" in conversations you've had with others?

Chapter 4

1. What tradeoffs do you see related to the following idea: You can be right, or you can be happy—choose one.

2. Watch "The Power of Vulnerability" TED Talk. What themes from Brené Brown's talk speak to you most deeply? (Go to www.ted.

com/talks/brene_brown_on_vulnerability.)

3. When have you experienced a lack of our most basic human need—connection—in your life?

Chapter 5

1. What does the distinction between "balance" and "centeredness" mean to you?

2. What are your most profound "used-to-thinks"—and what was involved in your process of discovering them?

3. What might happen if you were willing to reconsider something that you absolutely believe is true—even for a moment?

Chapter 6

1. How would you describe your relationship with conflict? Do you do everything you can to avoid it? Do you understand its value? Do you create it intentionally? What might be different for you if you had a different relationship with conflict?

2. What are your triggers—things that bring

about conditioned responses? What situations (people, places, events, etc.) are most likely to trigger you?

3. Have you considered the role you play in triggering others (children, spouses, employees, neighbors, etc.)? What if you were more intentional in your approach to communication—and honored your desire to stop triggering others?

Chapter 7

1. What might change in your daily life when you have the awareness that each person is struggling with some form of suffering?

2. Are there times and places where a simple act of compassion and empathy (the act of just rubbing someone's feet) has profoundly affected you?

3. Stop, take a moment, and consider someone else's story. What insights can you draw from the past that are related to someone's reaction in a situation?

Chapter 8

1. Have you ever considered—by relative percentage—the tiny percentage of our DNA that is related to appearance? What does this insight trigger for you?

2. How do you feel about the idea that we innately and unconsciously separate and categorize when it comes to "other" people?

3. Are there other examples in which you've seen yourself or others around you humanizing "the other" through shared experiences (as in the story about the New York subway above)?

Chapter 9

1. How good are you at choosing the energy you bring into a situation? If it's easy, why? If it's difficult, how come?

2. Are you naturally able to take on a "beginner's mind" when you start to learn something new? Or do your biases and conditioned ways of thinking get in the way?

3. How does the provocative description of the

Good Samaritan story make you feel? How likely is it that we might experience a version of that story today?

Chapter 10

1. Describe a situation where you've found yourself in the midst of conflict because someone is defending a position as opposed to searching for deeper interests.

2. What has led up to our society's preference to *not* look for "both-and" answers and instead move toward "either-or" thinking?

3. What comes to mind when you consider the Building Bridges approach to get teenage girls to experience the heartbeat in one another?

Chapter 11

1. When you're in the midst of a challenging situation, what might happen if you were able to check the energy you're bringing and shift your energy to a more productive place?

2. What's your reaction when you think of the

words "humble" and "vulnerable"?

3. Are you able to regularly give of the purity of your attention to others, or are you more frequently distracted by something (such as emails, texts, Facebook postings, eavesdropping)?

Chapter 12

1. Have you found yourself in a truly toxic, dysfunctional situation (at home or at work)? What was your response?

2. How do you feel about the notion that shifting worldviews starts with us, individually? Are you the type who says, "As soon as you're done changing, everything will be fine"?

3. How open are you to the possibility that truly remarkable outcomes are possible even in the face of "evidence" that tells you it's impossible?

Chapter 13

1. Are you someone who finds yourself disappointed or frustrated when faced with

someone's imperfection (for example, bad service at a restaurant or an oversight by a coworker during a meeting)?

2. How do you feel about the notion that how you do anything is how you do everything? Can you "be" two different people in two different situations?

3. Do you believe that love is universal—in relationships (kids, spouse, friends), in business, in politics, with the environment—or is love something situational (it belongs here but not there)?

Other Titles by Bob Tipton

Jump!
Get Unstuck

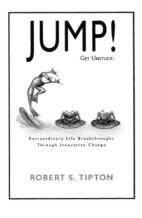

To get ahead, and stay ahead, it's time to foster and develop a new relationship with the status quo, the "deadly condition" that unfortunately continues to provide you with the same, old results. *JUMP!*, and its four stages of innovative change, will arm you with new insights, new approaches, and better tools to help you rapidly create more satisfaction, more joy, and more success in your life and in your organization.

JUMP!'s leadership fable, a tale of discovery and human triumph, is a compelling, inspiring story steeped in real-life wisdom. The *JUMP!* Innovative Change Model is a high-level yet comprehensive depiction of the tools and approaches used "behind the scenes" in the story.

Find *JUMP!* on Amazon and other book retailers.